First you slay the Dragon

First you slay the Dragon

Overcoming Leadership Myths

Jim Moore

First you slay the Dragon

Overcoming Leadership Myths

by
Jim Moore

Published by:
Moore Ideas, Inc.
Coppell, Texas

Printed in the United States of America

Cover art and page layout by
Ad Graphics, Tulsa, Oklahoma

ISBN: 0-9666626-2-8

ACKNOWLEDGMENTS

• • • • • • •

For all of the wonderful people,
too numerous to mention,
who have helped me these past years.

CONTENTS

• • • • • • •

INTRODUCTION

• • • • • • •

Myths

H is company had called Tom Bartini to a meeting. In the room that had been designated for the gathering sat over two hundred of Tom's peers. The Board of Directors had called this group together only two days ago. Tom was anxious to know what the meeting was all about. Oh, there had been rumors of some changes at the top; maybe they were going to announce the changes today.

All heads turned toward the door as the Chairman of the Board entered. Never a man for idle chatter, the Chairman quickly cut through the tension by getting right to the point. Everyone sat stunned as the Chairman announced that a new President was to be selected from the management present in the room today. Tom immediately was filled with excitement and anticipation. Tom knew he had an excellent chance of being named President. After all, Tom had been with the company the past twelve years in several key positions and had excellent evaluations. Tom knew he had all the qualities of a leader. His peers and supervisors had praised his intelligence and creative thinking. Tom was willing to take risks, but only after carefully analyzing the pros and cons of his eventual decision. High integrity and sensitivity toward his peers and subordinates were also among Tom's top qualities.

Tom knew no one else in the room was more courageous, committed, communicative, or change oriented than he was. Having been promoted often, Tom always used his newly acquired power wisely. Tom couldn't believe his good fortune. Today was going to be the payoff for all of his hard work and dedication.

The Chairman had allowed the buzz of excitement to permeate the audience, but now he was ready to announce his decision. The Chairman asked all of the two hundred managers to stand. Quickly, he told those in the group who were not the first born in their family to sit down. Then told all of those who were not male to sit. It was then that those not forty years of age or older were to sit down. Tom couldn't believe what he was witnessing. This is how he was picking our next President? The good news was that Tom was still standing. He was still in the running. Then Tom's world came crashing down; the Chairman announced that all those who were not six feet tall or taller must now sit down. Slowly and reluctantly Tom sat back down in his seat. Could the Chairman really pick the next leader of the company by these old myth standards? Tom knew the two people left standing. They did not measure up to him and lacked many of the qualities he knew were needed to give the company the new direction it sorely required. The Chairman then determined who of the two left standing came from the wealthiest family, and announced that he would be the next president/leader of the company.

By now you are aware that this story itself is a myth, that something like this set of non-value based decision making criteria, could not and would not have happened in our country today, and you would be correct. Unfortunately, many American businesses still deal with other forms of myths, which are equally subjective, equally destructive to morale, when it comes time to selecting their leaders.

Myths have been a part of our lives since time began. One of the most popular myths of all time is that of the Dragon. Homer used the mythical Dragon well in the *Iliad*; King Agamemnon had on his shield a blue, three-headed serpent. In England, before the Norman Conquest, the Dragon was chief among the royal ensigns of war. These colorful emblems were instituted by Uther Pendragon, father of King Arthur. Young men would be sent out to **"slay the dragon,"** the symbolic principle of evil, before knighthood was possible.

In present times, business myths are still prevalent and play a disruptive role. Promising Knights of Business must avoid these many myths, in particular, the ones that pertain to modern day leadership. They must not let antiquated myths distract them from applying good common sense practices that assure future success. Therefore, they must first seek to **"slay their dragons" by overcoming the myths that are still "in play" in business today.**

• • • • • • •

CHAPTER I

The Manager Versus The Leader
Leadership Characteristic Myths

As I travel around our country consulting with companies and observing other people, I have noticed a tendency to promote leaders by the myth system. We are still promoting the people who make us the most money. We are promoting the best controllers in the organization.

We promote to leadership positions the managers who are good at inventorying, budgeting, scheduling, problem solving, and controlling. The myth that great profit makers will also be great leaders is not necessarily correct. There are fundamental differences between a good manager and a good leader.

Good managers do all the essentials well. They are good at organizing and controlling. Managers make sure that few risks are taken in their organizations. Our fictional characters, in the introduction, used the myth system of ancient times to select the leader in that room.

If we had selected our leaders in more modern times by this same myth system, we would not have had the leadership of Mahout Ghandi, Margaret Thatcher, Winston Churchill, Henry Kissinger, and many of the CEO's in The United State companies today.

There is a fundamental difference between being a good manager and being good leader. Managers maintain order in business. Leaders create direction for a company, an association, and a business. Leaders have the flexibility to change that direction when it's needed. They intuitively understand what I tell the companies I work with in strategic and operational planning; "Your plan is your plan, until you change it!" Too often leaders feel married to their plan just because they created it. Leaders also gather all of their constituents around their plan, and then inspire them to do their very best to meet that plan and its objectives. They understand the means of building momentum and excitement around a strategic direction.

Therefore, leaders take risks and <u>create change</u>, while managers <u>maintain order</u>.

Operational Contrast

Managers (Plan by:)	Leaders (Set direction by:)
• Working in short time frames'	• Operating in the long term
• Analyzing	• Being inductive
• Preventing risks	• Taking risks
• Maintaining order	• Creating change
(the result) – **organization**	(the result) – **visualization**

Are the disciplines of management you have learned since you started with your company wrong? No; strong, effective management is very important. However, challenges of today call for more leadership than ever before. If companies have nothing but management, they strangle themselves and growth ceases. On the other hand, if you have nothing but leadership and no management, you have chaos and confusion. We need more leadership in our lives, in our organizations, and all throughout business communities while we must continue to reward and cultivate good managers.

I could give you many examples of good leaders: Perhaps George Washington, Thomas Jefferson, Dwight Eisenhower, or Winston Churchill. Perhaps it would have more impact to tell you about the first leader I ever encountered.

Please come with me back many years ago. It's Armistice Day, November eleventh, 1953. Two undefeated Pennsylvania high school football teams are going to battle it out for the Western Conference Championship. I was a member of one of those squads, a skinny, 150-pound wide receiver. Our opponents were led by Sam Valentine, a monster of a middle linebacker, who was so good he would later go on to be an All-American for Penn State University

Led by Valentine, our opponents were ahead by two touchdowns at half time. When our team went back to our locker room we were despondent and defeated. We sat there with our heads down feeling very sorry for ourselves.

Then in the doorway stood our coach saying, "We can win this game! I believe in you! All we have to do is change our game plan. I want to know what you can do out there?" One by one he asked us each that question. As we responded, the assistant coaches changed some of the plays, and wrote them on a black board. Then our coach got to the last man, leaning up against a locker, a young sophomore center by the name of Gary Connors. Gary said, "Coach, I don't know whether this means anything or not, but Valentine is right over my nose when we put a flanker on the weak side." (It always bothered me that they called the weak side any side that I was on!) Gary went on to say, "When we put a flanker on the strong side, Valentine cheats over a step or two." Coach then said, "You know, we can take advantage of that by running our reverse off tackle. Jim, I want you to get over and get into Valentine's way. You don't have to knock him down." Whoa, that was a relief! The man outweighed me by 100 pounds, but I was only seventeen years old. Like most teenagers, I thought I was invincible. "I can do it!" I yelled out. Our coach went on to say "I believe in you. I know you can take these changes we made and win this game. You are the best team I have ever had." As we filed out of the door, past our coach, to go back on that field he shook each one of our hands and thanked us for our individual and specific contributions.

17

Soon the second half began. We had the ball deep in our own territory. Our quarterback, who was empowered to change the plays as he saw fit, saw that Valentine had indeed cheated over! He called that reverse and when the ball was snapped I ran over to where Valentine was. I ran so hard I tripped over one of my teammates, banged into Valentine and, to his surprise (and more to mine), he fell down!

When he got up, he had the meanest, most evil look I had ever seen in my young life. He said to me (I'm going to clean this up for you), "Nice block kid, but if you ever come near me the rest of the game, I'll tear your head from your body!" I believed him! When I ran off of that field I looked at our quarterback and said, "Maybe we shouldn't run that play anymore!"

Our quarterback looked at me like I was the craziest person he had ever met. You see, we had scored a touchdown on that play, and five or six more times in the game our quarterback called that play. Five or six more times I ran over to where Valentine was and five or six more times Valentine came very close to reaching his objective. By the end of the game I was a mess, but it didn't matter because the score was 28-21 and we had won! Now, all of these years later, it's not the score or who won that I have the fondest memories of: It's the memories of our coach, our leader who believed in us. Our coach, who set the original direction for us, and had the flexibility to change that plan when it was needed.

Our leader had the courage to ask and to trust the opinions of 17-and 18-year-old kids. He gathered us around the new plan, and had us believing in it, by involving us in the change. He inspired us by believing in our abilities and, more importantly, by thanking each of us for our individual and specific contributions. Incidentally, that leader was my dad.

Basic Equipment For Leaders

Successful life in the business world is much like that football game played years ago. The need for change occurs, new direction is developed and communicated, employees are inspired and motivated to reach new goals. With the marketplace changing so rapidly, the leadership of our country's businesses will have to be ready to embrace change. Fight it and it will overpower you.

Operational Contrast Examples

Managers (Plan by:)	**Leaders** (Set direction by:)
• Weekly schedules	• One to five year plans
• Studies cost trends	• Estimates trend outcomes
• Puts cost controls in place	• Reposition a product line
• Sees that policy or procedure are followed	• Changes policy, specifications
(the result – expected day to day routine)	(the result – new goals and objectives)

Overcoming The Myth:

Evaluate your management and leadership style by self-examination, and by asking others' advice and opinions. Where do you fit into the following chart?

	Weak	**Strong**
Strong **Leadership**	Joe Smith (1)	(4)
Weak	Bob Green (2)	Susan Brown (3)

Management

19

Do you know anyone who belongs in box number 1? Let us take a look at Joe Smith. Joe is very strong on leadership, but weak in management. Joe has many great ideas, and tries to carry them out all at once. Joe comes up with a new program every week, and puts them into operation before the other programs are completed.

Everything Joe sees or reads he gets excited about, and wants to put these new ideas into his business immediately. Joe is continually creating havoc in his organization. The constant change is upsetting to everyone else in the company. Because no one has time to complete projects, moral takes a big drop.

Then there is Susan Brown who is in box number 3. Susan got ahead by being the number one moneymaker in her company. Susan has the ability to keep tight control over her operations, and knows where everything is at any time. If anyone has a problem, they bring it to Susan. However, Susan has no idea what the company really is, where it is going, or how it is going to get there. Susan brings no planning skills to the organization, no vision; she is only interested in the "bottom line."

Unfortunately, you have seen people like Bob Green. Bob can fit into box number 2 perfectly. Bob can neither lead nor manage. Bob needs to seriously evaluate if he is in the correct occupation.

Sadly, we also find it hard to locate people who fit into box number 4. Strong leaders, able to set direction and inspire others, while at the same time having good, reasonable control of their responsibilities. Is it your goal to be a well-balanced manager and an effective leader? Place yourself in one of these boxes. List why you are in the category, and what you must do to attain your goal. Now put your plan into action. Do not stop dreaming after you put your plan into motion. Circumstances change. Markets change. Employees change. You will need to be constantly looking ahead to challenges of tomorrow.

> *"It is never very clever to solve problems.*
> *It is far cleverer not to have them."*
> E. F. Schumacher

• • • • • • •

CHAPTER II

From Dream To Vision
The Myth Of Visionary Development

Y ou must have heard the term, "changing for change sake," at some point in your life. This saying, about change, has often been used by someone when complaining about an unwanted direction or decision that could effect his or her life. This attitude is usually caused by not having all the facts concerning the eventual outcome of the goals or vision of the persons responsible for the recommend or imposed change. Much has been written and said about "vision." It is often thought in order to have vision one must be born extremely creative. Well, being born with the basic need to create and research certainly helps, but to create vision for yourselves, your companies and organizations takes much more. Leaders have the ability to ask basic and pertinent questions.

To challenge the "way we have always done it." To make others think "is there another way we could get this done?" To create vision, leaders must listen well and be well read. Leaders must be able to use this information to make decisions and formulate strategies. It is certainly a myth that leaders do not dream. Dreams are an important element in creating your future. Your ideas, ideals, and dreams combine to form your goals that help create your visions.

Dreams are often looked upon negatively because they are confused with fantasy. People may have sexual fantasy, or they dream of winning the lottery. They use fantasy as a form of mental entertainment to help reduce stress. There is an important difference between fantasy and dreams. Fantasy can be used as a temporary relief from our troubles; dreams are your goals for the future.

Most of us dream of a better life for our families and ourselves. We must focus these visions into working goals. We all have ideas of what we want out life, work, and relationships. Putting your visions and goals into a working lifestyle will not only enable you to have a successful career, but will allow you to have the lifestyle you dream for yourself and your loved ones.

Every morning I take a brisk walk. This time alone is an excellent opportunity for me to review my needs, goals, and desires. It is a time to be creative and to dream. I'm not the only one who sets time aside for this kind of thinking. Many famous leaders and inventors used "creative time" in their daily routines.

Not long ago my wife, Anna, and I stopped at Thomas Edison's home in Ft. Myers, Florida. During the tour of the grounds a well informed guide told us that Mr. Edison loved to sit on his pier with a fishing pole, but no hook or bait. This time on the pier was reserved for dreaming. Thomas Edison had over one thousand patents in his life. Many of those ideas probably originated on that pier.

Leaders are seldom inflexible. If the leader is involving others and listening to other members of his or her organization on a regular basis, the need for change and flexibility will be obvious. Be careful not to use only your past experiences and successes as your criteria for making future directions. Circumstances are sure to change and your past wins can turn into tomorrow's losses. Be aware of the brilliant leader with strong opinions, they could lose out to the average person with the stronger thirst of knowledge.

Dreams, to become reality, must be taken from the creative process in your mind to the pragmatic stage where causes, effects, needs and results reign. Therefore, before reading on further, take a few minutes to think about your present goals for your career, and your personal life.

Your dreams may be that promotion you are looking forward to at work, or they might be that trip you have often dreamed about. Your dreams may be difficult to reach or possibly simple pleasures that would make you happy. I always wanted to learn how to juggle, but somehow never got around to learning. I finally put my mind to it, and included learning how to juggle as one of my 1997 goals.

I went to a novelty store and found that they not only sell juggling balls but instructional videotape as well. I talk about setting goals in one of my seminars, "Building a Career – Building a Life." Now my audience is surprised when, in the middle of a presentation, I start to juggle.

Give some thought to what you would like to accomplish in the next twelve months, and list your goals below.

MY GOALS FOR _____ ARE:

1. _____

2. _____

3. _____

4. _____

5. _____

6. _____

7. _____

8. _____

9. _____

10. _____

Doug Cavanaugh, founder and President of Ruby's Restaurant Group (a fantastic group of fifties diners), believes that the most important ingredient of reaching your dreams is never losing sight of your vision. Doug had a dream that California was ready to embrace a sparkling clean restaurant that served great food with lots of fun. His first unit was a tremendous success. Doug has never lost sight of his original goals as he continues to grow his company into a major chain.

"If man does not keep pace with his companions, perhaps it is because he hears a different drummer. Let him step to the music which he hears, however measured or far away."
Henry David Thoreau

• • • • • • •

CHAPTER III

Mistakes

The Myth That Great Leaders Seldom Make Mistakes

Mistakes happen. Anytime people are making decisions, choices or selections, incorrect solutions will inevitably occur. That's OK!

Great leaders analyze their decisions to see where they went wrong. They learn from their mistakes and go on from there. The business world sometimes punishes the people who have previously made mistakes, and rewards the error-free executive. Watch out for the errorless person; when they make their mistakes it may mean disaster for your company.

Had I believed in this myth system of business, or even known about it when I was planning on going to college, I probably would not have entered into management. When it was important to come from families of wealth in order to be a leader, I came from a poor family from the Pennsylvania Allegheny Mountains. There was, however, one myth I did believe in. I believed that successful leaders rarely ever made a mistake. Oh, if they did, they were little ones, and hardly visible.

Very quickly in my career I dispelled that myth. I was assigned as an Assistant Manager to Stouffer's Top of the Sixes in downtown Manhattan. I was an ambitious young man who wanted to get ahead. I realized that I would have to be noticed in order to get ahead. It was not long before I was given my chance to shine.

I was selected to serve the very first flaming Crepe Suzettes the Stouffer Foods Corporation was ever going to prepare. I walked into our gorgeous dining room that day to discover my very first customer was none other than Ethel Merman, the famous Broadway musical star. Do you remember Ethel Merman? She was the star of many great musicals 'Annie, Get Your Gun' was one of them. Oh, she was famous. I really wanted to do a good job for Miss Merman. Being perfect in front of Miss Merman was all I could think of as I got my pan hot, lined up my ingredients. Soon the pan was really hot; I took the butter and added it to the skillet. The butter popped and sizzled and steam curled into the air. Then I got the sugar and quickly made a sauce, spreading it all throughout the pan. I then got a large orange, cut it in half, and squeezed it into the pan. Oh, that sweet, acidic aroma that rose and filled the dining room.

All eyes turned in my direction; I was going to be a star! I could see the New York papers the next day, the Broadway columnists would write, "Restaurant Manager Lights Broadway Star's Fire!" The pan was now hot enough. I took the crepes and lined the bottom. Then I took the brandy and poured it over the ingredients.

Those of you who are familiar with flambé items know that in making flaming Crepe Suzettes you need to have sauce hot enough to produce a great flame. I took the bottle of brandy and poured some more; oh, what the heck a little more wouldn't hurt! Now I had the pan full to the top of hot, bubbling liquid. Slowly, I turned the pan toward the blue-orange flickering flames and BOOM! Something shot past me! Flames smoke and noise and more smoke...a lot of smoke.

I started blowing and waving away the smoke, but my first thought was for my customer Ethel! But where the heck was she? Then I saw her through the smoke; strangely, no one else was looking at her! Everybody else was looking up. Oh boy, there was a very large hole now in the ceiling. There was a smaller but significant hole now in the carpet. And an even smaller, but even more significant hole in Ethel's beautiful mink coat.

I didn't know what to do! I wanted to run, I wanted to hide, I wanted to blame it on somebody else, but I couldn't! I was the only dummy still standing there with a pan in my hand and, if you needed more proof of who the culprit was, guess who was the only one in that dining room with no eyebrows! Everyone was gathered around Miss Merman. Her face was turning red, green, and purple, her arms were flailing! All I thought of was how I wanted to get the heck out of there and, with all of the attention going to Miss Merman, I saw my chance. I snuck down the hallway to the manager's office, an office I knew I would never get to use. You see, my job was over, my career was over and, maybe if I was lucky, my life was over!

I stood in that office for what seemed like a long time. All of a sudden the door flew open and there stood Miss Merman. "Well, kid, how do you like show business so far? Ah, cheer up – now you have something to tell your grandchildren. You'll be laughing at this for years to come!" Then she turned and slowly walked away. Well, I learned a lot from Miss Merman that day. I learned to laugh at my mistakes and put them behind me. Yes, I learned not to fill the pan so full also. Most importantly I learned to learn from my mistakes, and to be patient with others who make them around me. Then I went on in my career to make hundreds, no, thousands of mistakes. Some how I still got promoted. Now, many years later, I am writing this book and speaking across the country to share my mistakes with others.

As leaders, you will make mistakes. After all, you are only human. However, if you want a leadership role, there is no escaping the fact that errors and their consequences will follow. Regardless of how long you may study a situation or potential opportunity before making your final decision, there is no guarantee of success. The factors that helped you make your decision may have changed, or you simply may have come to an inaccurate conclusion.

Beware of inactivity due to the fear of being wrong or making a mistake. I call it "freezing in the headlights of progress." You are apt to make more costly mistakes by inactivity. I once had a boss who hated to make decisions. His favorite line was "No decision is a decision, you know." Our company never reached it's potential due to his indecisiveness.

Many businesses have failed because management was frightened of making mistakes. I often told our company's management "The mortal enemy of progress is procrastination."

Leaders must have patience with those around them who make mistakes. If your subordinates are accepting responsibilities given to them by you, there will be times when they will make mistakes in fulfilling those duties. It is vital you support them at these times, and help them analyze what went wrong. They need your counsel in assisting them on alternative measures that could have been set up. Second-guessing can be extremely harmful to a person's ability to make future decisions. The greatest enemy of empowerment is second-guessing others' decisions.

Overcoming The Myth:

Try not to be impatient. Test as much as possible before action is taken. Life is full of trial and error. Businesses should test before implementing, especially if capital and human resources are at stake. Testing is desirable so that if mistakes are made, they are the least costly. Many leaders get impatient, and don't wait to test. They know what should be done. Past successes do not guarantee future victories in rapidly changing markets. An idea or important decision should go through different stages before put into action.

Progress Of A Decision

Idea ⟶ Idea sharing ⟶ Idea development ⟶

Pros/Cons ⟶ Cost benefit analysis ⟶ Concept fine tuning ⟶

Communication ⟶ Test ⟶ Roll out

Keep a record when mistakes are made. Write down what went wrong, and what could have been done differently. Share your mistakes with others within the organization. Help prevent others from making the same errors by being humble and open. (It is disconcerting to find there are leaders who spend an inordinate amount of their time convincing others the mistakes they made are really not their fault.) Just as important, keep records of your victories. It is equally valuable to you to understand why you have succeeded.

Live with your mistakes when they happen. Know that you have the ability to make mistakes, and own up to them. Taking risks will result in mistakes no matter how carefully the odds have been reduced. You serve no useful purpose getting down on yourself when things go wrong. Learn from your mistakes, and go on with your life and your business.

"Only those who dare to fail greatly
can ever achieve greatly."
Robert F. Kennedy

CHAPTER **IV**

• • • • • • •

Enthusiasm Versus Dignity
The Myth About Leadership Behavior

W e are born onto this earth with our own unique personalities, strengths and limitations. We are potential leaders. Parents, relatives, friends, teachers, and eventually bosses all attempt to mold our behavior. Most of us are given a message: that, to get ahead in the world, we must behave in a certain conservative fashion. Our enthusiasm for life is modified, controlled. Our basic qualities that we were born with are managed by others to fit what they believe is right or best for us. Leaders have different and various personalities, but they all have one thing in common. Leaders have a tremendous enthusiasm for their work, their life, and the people around them.

The other evening while having dinner with some friends I was asked how I managed to maintain my high level of enthusiasm with all the traveling I must do. They thought it must be very stressful having to travel constantly to share my experiences. I thought about this question for some time before replying. Perhaps I display a vast amount of enthusiasm in my life because I am aware the more enthusiastic I am the happier I feel. I'm not talking necessarily about the same amount of enthusiasm you see in a cheerleader at a football game. I'm talking about the enthusiasm you see in someone's eyes, you feel in their heart, that is displayed in their courage.

Enthusiasm isn't just an outward display of emotion; it's an invisible ingredient that races through your blood stream and prevents you from feeling tired or "down."

- Enthusiasm creates energy

- Energy creates passion

- Passion creates greatness

Remember when you were little and needed eight to ten hours of sleep each night? If you didn't get your required night's rest you would get up grumpy and tired.

Remember the one night – perhaps the night before your first day of school, or your first vacation trip with your parents, or maybe the first visit to the carnival. On this night, for some reason, you only received five hours of sleep, but you awoke very excited and full of anticipation. You couldn't wait to get going and you weren't tired. You were enthusiastic.

In this competitive environment we live in, enthusiasm is vital. If we don't have enthusiasm, someone else will. Whether it's a team of people or just you, don't let someone else have more enthusiasm.

I am reminded of an old story that makes this point so well. A weary fellow decided to retire and move to Virginia. He moved to Virginia because he had a friend there with a pig farm.

He bought his own farm, closed the deal, and was sitting on his porch rocking away when he thought, "You know, I've got a farm, I should raise something." He thought about his friend went down to the market, and he bought a parcel of pigs.

He also bought a brand new truck, threw the pigs in the truck and brought them home, only to discover that he had bought nothing but female pigs. Now, I don't have to tell you he isn't going to raise many pigs that way. So what to do?

He called his friend and his friend said, "Bring them on down to my farm." He threw the pigs in the truck and down they went. When he got there, they did what little boy and little girl pigs will do when they get together. When it was over, my friend said to his friend, "How do I know if this took?"

The friend said, "It's easy. Tomorrow morning if they are grazing on the grass, you'll know it took."

So the next morning, our friend woke up with much enthusiasm and anticipation. He ran to the second story window, looked out and saw that his pigs were not grazing on the grass. Darn! He called his friend up and said, "They are not grazing on the grass." His friend said, "Bring them on down again!" So he threw them in the truck and down they went. The next morning, with the same great enthusiasm and anticipation, our friend got out of bed and raced to the window...they still weren't grazing on the grass! He threw them in the truck and down they went once more! This went on for ten days.

On the eleventh morning, our friend had lost his enthusiasm. In fact, he rolled over, looked at this wife and said, "Honey, I can't stand it anymore! Will you go check on those lousy pigs?" His wife got out of bed, put on her slippers and padded over to the window and looked out. She looked back at her husband and said, "Well, they're not grazing on the grass, but they're all loaded in the truck, and one of them is honking the horn!"

Don't give that enthusiasm up; don't give it to someone else. Enthusiasm can easily be transferred. Corporate America, for years, has had an image for executives to up hold. Dress for success. Behave with proper etiquette. Show little emotion. Keep your sense of humor under control. No one can argue against the wisdom of this behavior. However, by attempting to act as is expected, we tend to dampen our basic enthusiasm. Do not get caught in the atmosphere of what others expect a leader to be. Be you, have fun, and help others to enjoy their role in the company. The "dignified" executive is the one who is in touch with his/her people. Dignity is honesty of oneself.

Overcoming The Myth

How can you handle the need to maintain your dignity, and still be enthusiastic? For years my peers and mentors would caution me to maintain my dignity. My actions should always represent my position in the corporation. Their caution and concern did little to dampen my zeal for my work but, no doubt, did keep my outward enthusiasm bottled up to a degree. Then I started my speaking and seminar business. I did as much speaking as I could in front of my peers who were much more experienced than I did.

Every time I spoke I would ask them to evaluate my performance. When analyzing their comments, it became clear to me that one area stood out as a need for improvement. I needed more energy. My presidential manner was showing. I decided to hire a coach, Sarah Reeves of Newport Beach, California. Sarah's objective was to assist me in overcoming my negative energy impressions. Sarah helped me work on my voice, mannerisms, positioning, and story content with increased positive energy as our goal.

Sarah did a wonderful job in all the aspects we worked to improve, but one comment made all the difference in the world to me. Sarah told me "Jim, when you are on up there on stage, you are there for your audience, not for you." All of a sudden, like a bolt of lighting, it came to me. There isn't anything I can't do on that stage. As long as what I do will help my audience see the point I am attempting to make. You are leading not for yourself, but for others.

"The thrill of victory or the agony of defeat are
overshadowed by the experience of giving it your all."
Bobby Moore

• • • • • • •

CHAPTER V

What Compels Us To Want To Slay The Dragons?
The Myths About Leaders Basic Needs

Know your present needs. Throughout your life the factors (needs) that drive you continue to change. How often we come up with these new needs depends on the individual, but I think the changes come around every ten years or so. When I started in the business world, I was driven by the need to succeed, to be recognized for my efforts and results, and to have power and authority. It would be safe to say that career, money, and security was the dominant needs of all my peers in that era. Now my needs have changed. I am much more driven by my need to be with my family, and the need to share my knowledge with others. I have found that over the year's people, in mass, shift the priority of their needs.

Our research of "Generation X" indicates that this eighteen-to thirty-five-year old segment has totally different needs than that of the baby boomers. This generation despises being branded by any name. They resent being thought of as Bart Simpson or Wayne and Garth. They are individuals and work hard to maintain that individuality. Generation-Xer's are not loyal to any company. They have seen their parents work all their life for a firm only to be down sized in their advanced years. The Generation X group are fun loving but conservative. They want to enjoy life, their job, and their surroundings. Family is much more important to the X-generation than it was to the preceding generation. The X-Generation has a negative view of the world.

This generation has watched more TV and, as a result, has probably witnessed more violence than any generation in history except for those involved in a war. They do not believe that social security or Medicare will be available to them. On the other hand, this generation believes they will prosper in the world and be successful in business. They are personally optimistic, but institutionally cynical. The Generation-Xer's have been educated with technology and are, by far, the best educated generation in history. By the year 2000, for the first time in the history of the world, the young will be educating the old. It is as important for the older generation to understand the needs of the "new employees" as it is for the generation entering the work force to know their own needs.

Though we are driven by needs, we are born with certain basic strengths and limitations that have an effect on our behavior. We have no control over these needs. Needs were given to us by the mysteries that cause our different personalities. Before I go any further, it is important for you to know that I am not a doctor, nor do I have any degrees in psychology. I am simply relating my beliefs based on the experiences I have had with hundreds of people, in my business life, over these past thirty plus years.

There is a company in Houston, Texas, called Management Technologies, Inc. that sponsors the theory that people are born with four basic needs.

1. AUTHORITATIVE / DECISIVE
   - Short-term tangible outcome
   - Progress
   - Activity

2. ADAPTIVE / COOPERATIVE
   - Supportive community
   - Flexibility
   - Feedback

3. CREATIVE / DEVELOPMENTAL
   - Understanding
   - Alternative choices
   - Time to reflect, consider and create solutions

4. METHODICAL / ANALYTICAL
   - Consistency
   - Structure or Patterns
   - Control and order

These basic needs produce "walking around" needs that we use, in varying degrees, every day. How we use and prioritize these needs depends greatly on our "born" needs and the environment in which we have lived the past ten years.

Examples Of "Walking Around" Needs:

1. POWER

2. RECOGNITION

3. CONTRIBUTION

4. CAREER

5. MONEY

6. SECURITY

7. FAMILY

8. QUALITY OF LIFE

9. FAITH

10. RESPONSIBILITY

11. COMMUNITY

Please take a few minutes at this time to select the five- (5) needs that are most important to you at this time in your life.

1. _____

2. _____

3. _____

4. _____

5. _____

These are the important "walking around" needs that drive you. They are the incentives that get you out of bed each day, make you happy, and give you purpose. Would you please now select your three (3) most important needs out of the above.

1. _____

2. _____

3. _____

I am sure you found this a little harder to do than the previous exercise. Here is an even more difficult request. Please select the number one (1) need that is most important to you today.

1. _____

Are you surprised at your decision? Perhaps not, but whatever your final determination was will affect your life, your decisions, and those around you until you find another need has taken its place.

My research has come to some interesting conclusions on what the general sense of the population is moving toward, with respect, to a common need. In all of the "Build a Career – Build a Life" seminars I have conducted 89.7% who completed this exercise have chosen family or quality of life as their number one need. People today want to get ahead, want to reach their career objectives and are not afraid to work. They just do not want to sacrifice their family or their perception of their standards to obtain their dreams.

The Relationship Of "Born Needs" To "Walking Around" Needs

Interestingly, it is possible to match up the four basic "born" needs with the "walking around" needs. Since we are all individuals with different backgrounds, experiences, and priorities we compensate our basic needs with how we act. We use different needs when things are going great and we are the happiest. However, when we are under stress, we fall back on other needs to help us through those times. Frequently, we can see the correlation between our "born" and our "walking around" needs.*

AUTHORITATIVE / DECISIVE

Power

Responsibility

Recognition

ADAPTIVE / COOPERATIVE

Family

Community

Quality of life

---

* Tony Alessandra, Ph.D., and Michael J. O'Connor, Ph.D. have recently published a book titled The Platinum Rule. This interesting book discusses in much more depth the theory that we all are made up with varying degrees of four basic styles. I recommend this book for part of your library.

CREATIVE / DEVELOPMENTAL

Career

Faith

Contribution

METHODICAL / ANALYTICAL

Money

Security

A very successful CEO once confided to me that he felt he would have to let his head of operations go. This CEO was saddened by his decision since the operations person was an employee of good standing, and had been with his organization a long time. When I inquired why he suddenly felt this way I discovered an interesting situation. Yes, it was true that the operations head was not having one of his better years. Sales and profits were behind budget, but this was not a trend. It was the first time in five years negative results were occurring.

I discovered that both the CEO and the Operations Head were under stress, and that each person had a different management style. The CEO was really more upset about how the Operations head was going about solving the negative trends than with the trends themselves. The CEO was a "task-oriented, get things done in a hurry" type of manager, while the Operations Head was a more "methodical, get your ducks all in a row" type of person. Once I was able to show the CEO that they were both attacking the same problem, but with different styles, he was able to concentrate on assisting the Operations Head rather than criticizing out of frustration.

"Every man of action has a strong dose of egotism, pride, hardness and cunning. But all those things will be forgiven him, indeed, they will be regarded as high dualities, if he can make them the means to achieve great ends."
Charles de Gaulle

• • • • • • •

CHAPTER VI

The Goal Versus The Basic Function

The Myth Concerning The Basic Function Of A Leader

I come across many interesting people in my travels. It doesn't matter whether they are financial bankers, business executives, academics, or retail employees. I like to ask them these questions: What is your goal and what is your company's basic function? What is your company's reason for being? Almost always I am told the company's reason for being is to make money or to increase stockholder value.

Making money and increasing the value of stockholders is very important; in fact, it is essential. But it is not or should not be your company's basic function. The basic function of a company must be to create and keep customers. Customers are the lifeblood of an organization; without them there can be no sales and without sales there can be no profit. Please don't go to work tomorrow and tell your boss you just read a book that says we don't need to make money anymore. Making money is very important; but it should be your goal, not your basic function. A Company needs to make money to pay back its investors. An organization needs profit to invest in future growth. What often happens is companies confuse these goals with their basic function. When this happens, management and employees become the enforcers of rules and policies. The same standards hold true for the leaders of these companies.

The leaders' basic function is to create and keep customers not to make money. And each individual within that company, regardless of their position, has frequent opportunities to display their leadership characteristics. Their leadership qualities show every time an employee comes in contact with a customers.

Not long ago I was on a speaking tour that took me away from home for over two weeks. My return trip found me arriving home at the airport on a Sunday around 2:00 p.m. My wife picked me up and started driving toward our home. I was too tired to go to a movie or go out for dinner so I suggested we stop at a video store, which we did. I don't care to share with you the name of the video store, but I'll give you a hint: it sounds a lot like "Clockduster." My wife and I selected our two videos and proceeded to the front where a very nice, smiling young lady awaited us. "Good afternoon sir," she greeted me. I handed her my videos and my membership card. After running my card through the computer the young lady looked at me with sad eyes. "Oh sir, do you know that you owe a $4.63 penalty for a late return of past videos?"

I have been coming to this particular store for two years and have, on more than several occasions, paid a penalty even when I thought I had returned my videos on time. Because of this experience, I now keep a record of my returns and so I was absolutely positive I had returned these videos on the designated due date. It was only natural for me to say, "Young lady, I am 100% positive I returned those videos on time. This has happened to me before in this store. You people must have made mistakes logging the returns. What is the matter with all of you?"

She looked at me and then around us to make sure no one was looking. "You know sir, we get so many complaints about this, I don't know what the matter is here." Looking around again, she went on, "In fact, the other day they charged me for a late return and I know that I got mine back on time." I was relieved to hear her say that.

"Now that you can understand my frustration, would you please credit me for the $4.63?" "Oh no sir, I can't do that, I have to get a manager." The manager was the last person I wanted to see at that time for I was tired and all I wanted was my credit, my videos, and to go home.

Out came the manager looking at me as if I was there for the sole purpose of cheating him out of his hard-earned revenues. "What seems to be the problem here?" he said. "Well sir, it's like this, you claim I owe $4.63 for not returning my videos on time and I distinctly remember returning the videos on time. You have made a mistake and I would like to be credited for the $4.63." He replied, "The computer says you owe $4.63." "I know what the computer says," I retorted. "I don't care what the computer says; I want a credit." He looked at me for a second or two before answering. "The computer never lies." he responded. By now I was starting to lose it. To make matters worse, my wife was standing behind me repeating, "Don't pay it, don't pay it." So I pulled out a five-dollar bill. While holding the bill in one hand and my membership card in the other, I said, "You see this five dollar bill? If you take it, you get my card back as well and I will never come back to any of your stores for the rest of my life."

He looked at me as if to say that won't be all that long, and took my five-dollar bill, handed me the change, and I promptly handed him my card which he accepted. As my wife and I walked out of the video store, I turned and said, "Not only will I not ever come back to shop in any of your stores again, I am going to tell everyone I can." Little did this manager know what I do for a living.

Since that incident I have told over 500,000 people. On one occasion, in Kansas City, over 100 people in the audience cut up their membership cards and gave them to me as a souvenir. Not too long ago, I received a call from a Regional Manager for that video company. Someone had told him about my story. He told me if I didn't tell that story anymore he would send me some free coupons. I replied that I would not quit telling that story because they had a lovely young lady they just didn't trust to make a decision. They also had a manager to whom they hadn't bothered to explain the company's real basic function. That manager still thinks it's to make money. Well they made money on me, $4.63 to be exact, but how much have they lost on the people I have told? What about all of the others that have been treated in this same fashion?

If this company does not discover its true mission and basic function, some savvy competitor will take a large share of its market away. The consumer has changed and therefore the marketplace has changed. The customer will not and cannot tolerate anything less than immediate satisfactory solutions to any problem they encounter. "Old time" service in a "new time" market will only cause heartbreak. It happens everywhere. The worker, whether part of management or out on the sales floor, has the same basic function as the company, and that is to create and keep customers.

We can understand very clearly that our goal to make money is essential. We need money for mortgages, rent, food, clothing, and transportation. We must, however, not confuse our goal with our basic function, for if we do we have turned our company's mission into nothing but a slogan.

Recently, I was working with a cafeteria company, helping the individual stores do marketing plans. I asked a General Manager what his single biggest challenge was? He replied that it was teaching his customers his stores' concept. I said "Oh and what is it you are teaching your customers?" He replied, "Well, when they come down the line, and they want more than one or two entrees, I must tell them that our policy is they can have only two entrees the first time through the cafeteria line. I said, "Young man, your customers understand your concept perfectly. It is you who do not understand your concept, because outside that door it says 'All You Can Eat.' He had turned into a policeman, not a leader, because of profit and food cost percentage. He was driven by the dollar, not by the customer. In this case, the customer knew what the concept was, he didn't.

A few years ago I was the president of a dinner-house chain in California. I was standing in one of our restaurants in Anaheim, California, with the manager on a busy Saturday night. We had people in the lobby and the dining rooms were full. Out of the corner of my eye, I saw a table of four people: a man and a woman with two children. Seated with their parents were a little boy, about ten years old, and a little girl, about eleven or twelve. They seemed to be having a good time, except the little girl had a pout and a tear coming down her cheek.

She was very unhappy and, just when I noticed her, our server came by, took a look at her and said, "You don't look like a happy camper. Is there anything wrong?" The little girl didn't hesitate; she said, "I didn't want to come to this restaurant! I wanted to go over there!" and pointed out the window to El Torito, a Mexican restaurant. The server didn't bat an eye she looked at the parents for approval and said, "You know in the back we have some wonderful Hispanic cooks. If you just give me a moment I bet they will be glad to make you a great Mexican meal." The parents said okay, and the little girl said, "Yea!" with a smile starting to appear.

The server took off for the back with the manager and me right behind her. We were more than curious for we knew there was nothing in the house to make Mexican food; we were a steak house. We came around the corner just in time to see the server pull $10 out of her tip pocket and hand it to a busboy. She then said, "Will you go to El Torito and buy two enchiladas, a taco, rice and beans?" Here was a person who knew her basic function exactly. Oh, she knew we wanted her in the dining rooms all of the time. She also knew where she made her tips but, most importantly, she knew her basic function was <u>to create and keep customers.</u>

I am concerned with the company service policies that are solely centered on a motto: "The customer is always right." Many of the leaders of these companies merely make the statement and send a poster out. They may even tell a few Nordstrom stories and feel they have done all of the service training needed. In all reality, the customer isn't always right.

Employees know this fact and, without consistent training centered on creating customers, many employees will have the mentality, "If the customer is always right, this person must not be a customer because they are certainly wrong." Training your employees to treat people in a fashion that will keep them as customers even if they are wrong is a very important part of a leaders basic function.

The myths that confuse many leaders, as they attempt to guide their companies today, can be as misguiding as the ones that sent the Knights out to slay the dragons.

Most companies, I've observed, have mission statements of some sort. Too often these mission statements are thought up and published because "it's expected." The Board of Directors expects it or it's just a good thing to do. These are often the only reasons companies have these statements. There is no sincere desire by top management to live every day by the standards they have outlined. If management was sincere about living and working by their mission statement they wouldn't make some of the rules or "polices" they inflict on their customers.

Much too often companies have missions to be the best at whatever they do. They want to reach out and give the most wonderful service that can be provided to their customers. They say, "The customer is always right!" Then they turn around and mandate some rule that is so anti-customer, it drives their patrons away. Let me give you an example. A company develops a promotion to drive a certain segment of the market into their stores. A senior citizen discount is a good example. This promotion works, and thousands of seniors patronize the establishments.

The promotion is working so well that management gets concerned that some customers may be taking advantage of them by getting the discount when they are not fifty- five years of age or older. So, in order to control the one percent of the customers that may be "cheating" them, they put a senior card into effect and tell their managers not to give the discount to any one unless they show their card. This silly rule is control-oriented and inconvenient to ninety-nine percent of their customers, just for the sake of the other one- percent. Believe it or not, this kind of thinking is still prevalent in many businesses today.

There are some companies I know of that have mission statements they live by every single day. The mission statement of R&M Food Services, Inc., owned and operated by Rueben Villavicencio and his wife, Millie, is:

"Making our customers feel like valued guests."

"Servicing our guests in a loving, caring, and quality atmosphere."

"Providing good food and value."

Rueben and Millie believe in their mission. They teach their mission to every person who joins their company regardless of their position. Rueben, while visiting his restaurants, will ask employees if they can repeat the mission statement word for word. If the employee recites the statement correctly, they receive a five-dollar bill. Their restaurants, Millie's Restaurant and The Whole Enchilada, operate in California, and if you haven't eaten in them give yourself a treat.

Another interesting company is Rock Bottom Breweries out of Boulder, Colorado. They believe that "wonderful people working together; empowered to do what is right" is the key to their success. Their mission at Rock Bottom is "To run great restaurants with great people." If you have ever been to their restaurants you'll know it really works for them.

Overcoming The Myth:

It is really very simple to overcome the myth that a leader believes his or her reason for being is to make as much money as possible. Understand, believe, and carry out the principal concept that a leader's basic function is to create and keep customers. If leaders "walk the talk," their reward will be the profit goals they seek.

Once I had a boss, Vince Kikugawa, who had a slogan **"Pride before Profit**." Vince believed if we were proud of what we served, how we served it, and who served it, the profit would take care of itself. The premise of "Pride before Profit" is sometimes difficult for business people who are heavily into management-only styles. Everyone in an organization must live a principle, which states, "a business thrives on its customers:" for that to happen, they need leadership from the top of the organization. One northeastern seaboard company, which understands this principle, is the Tennaco Company, makers of quality ships. Over their front gates is a sign proudly displayed.

"We are in business to make good ships
at a profit – if we can
at a loss – if we must
but always – we will build good ships"

*"The worship of premium pricing always creates
a market for the competition."*
Peter Drucker

• • • • • • •

CHAPTER VII

One Leader Versus Many
The Myth Only One Person Can Be The Leader In A Group

Another rather prominent myth of leadership is that there can be no more than one leader in an organization, group or company. The rationale for this top-directed hierarchy ranges from, "This is the way we've always done it," to "I must be in control on a constant and continuous basis in order for all to go smoothly." The pyramid organizational chart that we grew up with and ever since have been using worked while our country went through the industrial age. Products and markets changed slowly while customer expectations did not. Past leaders would set up factories and tell people what they wanted done and everybody would follow those instructions. But times are changing and the marketplace is changing. Your customers are changing – what is happening? In two words, technology and computers.

When I first started in business, I was told that computers would change my life. Computers would make my life so much easier. I wouldn't have to work so hard! I was going to have so much more leisure time! How many of you are working fewer hours now than you did five years ago? I doubt many of you can answer that question in the positive. What has happened is that the computer and its components have created more work for us. It gives us more information, more data to analyze, more opportunities, and more problems to solve.

I have a friend on a college board who deals with speech pathology. She specializes only in cleft palates. She told me that she gets enough information on her desk, daily, through her computers and fax machines and other technical equipment, that if she read everything it would keep her busy for six months. The same phenomenon has happened to our customers. They are extremely pressed for time and time has become very precious to them. In 83.7% of the households in the United States today, two people are working just to maintain a standard of living that they were used to when they were growing up. Time has become precious and value has become a paramount issue. Your customers are not only pressed for time, they are also very value conscious. Customers want not only to pay a fair price for their purchases, they want immediate and attentive service. They do not want to hear, "I will have to go get a manager," or "That's against our policy." Customers want their problems solved immediately. That means that every one of your employees must have leadership skills in order to satisfy the customers' needs in a timely fashion.

Just before I left my former company to start up my own business, I decided to perform an experiment in Bakersfield, California. We had a Reuben's Steak house and Seafood Grill that was doing okay, making a little money. However, we wanted to see what the outcome would be if we took the Reuben's sign down and put a Charley Brown's sign up, did some redecorating, and had a crash course on creating and keeping customers. The concept change was very successful: sales were up 43 percent. Two weeks after we had opened, I received a phone call from a customer who said, "I want to tell you about my luncheon experience in your restaurant yesterday."

I don't have to tell you that when you get one of those calls, it usually is not going to be a pleasant experience. This gentleman went on to tell me that he had gone into the restaurant for lunch and ordered his food. Twenty minutes later his food still had not come, and he couldn't get anyone's attention. He then went out through the lobby and yelled at the hostess, "I'm never coming back to this place again." Then he got on the phone in his car and started calling his friends, telling them how bad Charley Brown's was. He told me that he stopped for gas and then ran a few errands. When he got to his office, waiting for him in the lobby was our hostess with his sandwich, that he had ordered, and a whole chocolate cake to apologize for his bad service. There was someone who knew what her basic function was. There was someone who showed leadership skills to make independent decision on how to create and keep customers. That customer told me he not only called his five friends back, he called many other friends to tell them how good our restaurant was. It wasn't I who won that customer back, I was in my office 180 miles away. That hostess won him back. An employee who had been trained, by the local management, that her basic function was to create and keep customers. Training in your culture and philosophy is vital when implementing and maintaining your standards.

Overcoming The Myth:

Trust your people to make the correct decisions. You felt good enough about them to hire them and keep them employed; you might as well trust their judgement. The key to this trust (empowerment, if you will) is training. Expect no one to understand your culture, your goals, and your objectives without proper and consistent training. Consider what it will take, in detail, to consistently deliver the message to all your people. Make sure that their training includes specific "hands on" experience. Test them to see that the program is thoroughly understood, and then implement your program. More can be done by many, which are skillfully trained, than by a lone individual giving orders to the uninformed.

Encourage all your people to know themselves well. People who understand their own strengths and limitations have the confidence to concentrate on important principles such as the basic function of their company and themselves. To effectively establish goals that will fulfill their dreams, their expectations for themselves, and get the most out of your potential, you must have working knowledge on your strengths and your limitations. Leaders are aware of their capabilities, and are continuously seeking ways to capitalize on their strengths and improve their limitations.

*"He was one of those men who possess almost every gift,
except the power to use them."*
Charles Kingsley

●●●●●●●

CHAPTER VIII

The Value Of Evaluation
Becoming The Man Or The Myth

T he ability for leaders to empower others takes certain characteristics. The leader who is comfortable sharing responsibility will be secure, trusting, willing to share credit, and to assume blame when failures occur. One of my favorite leaders is Joe Paterno, head football coach at Penn State University. I admire Joe more for his ability to state: "I made a mistake," than for the 300 victories he has accomplished. Joe Paterno is also honest and realistic. I once witnessed the number one team in the nation, Penn State, play an unranked Minnesota University team. Penn State was a 34-point favorite before this game. Minnesota played their hearts out only to make two critical mistakes that cost them the game. The final score was Penn State 16 – Minnesota 15. After the game Joe told the press, "We were out-coached and out-played, we just out-lucked them." No excuses, just an honest evaluation are what you can expect from this great leader.

Everyone has their own image of who they think they are. What we think we are is, of course, not as important as how we are measured by others. In order for leaders to guide others they must first have an honest assessment of themselves. The different approaches to an introspective evaluation of our strengths and limitations are:

Self-Evaluation

Self-Evaluation is available to us whenever we choose to use it. Thorough self-evaluation on a consistent basis can be very valuable when analyzing our victories and our defeats. No one of us should rely totally, however, on self-evaluation for we imperfect human beings often rationalize our defeats.

We forget to evaluate our victories, chalking them up to superior management or just our magnetic personalities. When I was operating restaurants on the east coast I noticed that my General Managers tended to explain good performances with "there is nothing like great management." However, poor performances would be explained by "it was that lousy snow."

Work Evaluation

Work evaluations are an excellent source to determine your strengths and limitations. Sadly, many companies still do not have a performance evaluation program or, if they do, have a program, they do not, adequately enforce it. If you are fortunate to be working in a company that does have a good evaluation program, be sure to take full advantage of the process. Ask questions when you are evaluated. How can you use your strengths to better serve the company and meet the business goals you have set for yourself? How can you best control your limitations? What will the response feedback arrangements show if progress is being made? Caution! Beware of self-rationalization. Often, you may rationalize your shortcomings instead of actively putting improvement plans together.

A few years ago I became vice president of operations for a large restaurant chain. While the Human Resources Department had an evaluation policy, no real evaluations had ever taken place. A correction of this insufficient practice was needed. After implementing the first wave of performance reviews, I sat with a Regional Manager who had been with the company over twenty years. His performance evaluation rating was poor. After explaining specifically what his deficiencies were, I gave him an itemized list of action steps that he must take for improvement. Two weeks later in a follow up meeting, I was astounded to find out that he was evaluating his own performance as "outstanding." I immediately set out to explore the matter further. Why was his self-evaluation so much better than the evaluation of his performance I had done just two weeks before? I came to this surprising finding. He agreed with my evaluation at the time of our original meeting. However, once he got into his car, and started to drive the 150 miles back to his home, he started to rationalize his shortcomings one by one. By the time he reached his destination, this manager had come to the conclusion that there were good reasons for his performance, and therefore he had no shortcomings. I learned to follow up on evaluations within two days.

The best favor you can do for yourself is to discuss your evaluation with your evaluator, come to a mutual agreement, and develop a plan for improvement. Leaders should attempt to improve their shortcomings not totally eliminate them. Everyone in your organization should be constantly on a self-improvement program, and aware of the leadership responsibilities they carry.

To improve your leadership skills, I suggest testing for your management style characteristics. There are many excellent companies that do this form of testing. The most cost-effective means to understanding how you act in normal everyday situations is to take the test on page 35 in the book "The Platinum Rule" by Tony Alessandra, Ph.D., and Michael J. O'Conner, Ph.D., published by Warner Books. Books may be purchased by writing Alessandra & Associates, PO Box 2767, La Jolla, CA 92038, TEL.1-800-222-4383. e-mail Keyspkr@aol.com

There is another excellent company I work with that specializes in managerial behavior. Management Technologies, Inc. 5847 San Felipe Ste. 650, Houston, TX 77057 TEL.713-784-4421. WEB SITE: www@manatech.com

Friends And Loved Ones

Our friends and loved ones will often help us in defining our strengths and limitations. You will find that approaching your friends with a straightforward question like, "Would you please list all my weaknesses" will often result in diluted responses. Friends and loved ones do not want to take the chance of losing your friendship and hurting your feelings. Friends will so often tell you what they think you want to hear. After all they love you the way you are.

A better approach might be to ask your friend or loved one, " I have been given a new assignment at work. Of all my strengths, which do you think will help me the most in completing this task, and what one thing do you think I could work on to help me do a great job on this assignment?" This is a less threatening approach to the subject, and will most often get you honest responses.

Mentors

Using mentors for learning and advice is an excellent idea. Mentors usually are able to help you with their knowledge, and often can advise the appropriate action you should take while taking into consideration your strengths and limitations.

My first mentor was a gentleman named Ted Swartz. Ted owned and operated a men's clothing store in Punxsutawney, Pennsylvania. For some reason Ted took a liking to me. Ted always found time to listen to my problems and to give advice when he was asked. I am sure I wasn't the only high school person Ted helped, but I let on that he was my own personal consultant. On Ted's advise I investigated the hospitality field, and found that I was well suited to pursue a career in what was, then, a fledgling industry. Thank you, Ted, for caring.

The summation of assisted and unassisted evaluation should give you an excellent introspective knowledge of yourself. Ask yourself, "What is my single best quality? What is my best skill? How can I use this best skill and quality so it will have the biggest impact on my life and my career?" Focus on using your best quality and skill.

You can have a tremendous impact on your life if you focus on your strengths. How can you, by focusing on your top talent, make a greater impact on your job? At home? In the community? By utilizing your best quality and best skill, how can you make an greater impact on your career and your life?

> *"A blind man knows he cannot see, and is guided,*
> *but he that is blind in his understanding, which*
> *is the worst blindness of all, believes he sees*
> *as the best, and scorns a guide."*
> Samuel Butler

• • • • • • •

CHAPTER IX

Motivation Versus Inspiration
The Myth Of How Leaders
Rally Their Troops

One of the biggest myths in business deals with leaders' ability or inability to motivate other people. During WWII, General Dwight D. Eisenhower was quoted as saying, "Leadership is getting other people to do what they never intended to do." Those were soldiers he was talking about. They either did what was ordered or were court martialed. They also had an extra incentive. Failure to follow orders could lead to your death in a war. Fifty years have passed since General Eisenhower allegedly made that statement, and times and people have changed. The truth is, leaders can not motivate anyone to do anything they do not want to do.

I recently held a seminar for a California-based retail company. I asked all of the attendees if they would "please raise their right hands." As you would expect, 100% of the audience complied with my request. I asked them why they all raised their hands and I got the following responses: "You said please," "It was easy to do," It didn't take much energy."

I then asked the audience to please go outside and run around the building three times. No one moved. I reminded them I had said please. It didn't matter; they were not going to do it because they just didn't want to. This is only one example but, it is my belief that leaders cannot motivate others. They can, however, inspire others. I like the word 'inspire' because it can be broken down into two words, "inner" and "spirit." It's the spirit that's inside us that creates the desire to do something.

A leader's role is to enhance others' self-esteem. Why is enhancing others' esteem so important? In the simplest of terms, people with high self-esteem do a better job. To establish this important environment of fostering self-esteem, leaders cannot rely solely on their instincts. Leaders must work hard, on a consistent basis, to avoid the common pitfalls that can erode self-esteem. How often has someone said to you – or you may have innocently said to one of your people – one of the following?

1. I don't think you're ready for this job, but give it a try.

2. You just don't seem to understand.

3. You should know better than to say that.

4. I thought you would have a greater sense of pride in your work.

5. If you would listen, you would understand.

6. You can't be serious about that suggestion.

7. Don't you think there's a better way to do it than the way you handled it?

8. I hope you are smart enough to know that.

9. I'm surprised to hear that from a person with your experience.

10. When you're as experienced as I am then you will understand.

11. I really thought you knew more than you do about this.

12. I just don't know how you can say that.

I am sure you can come up with many more phrases or statements that you have heard over the years that lower one's self-esteem. Just as it is important to avoid using statements that lower one's self-esteem, it is equally important to use words that enhance self-esteem.

The ways we can enhance self-esteem are endless but not ever practiced enough. Some of these ways are:

1. Praise specific task/job.

2. Give special assignments.

3. Give "OK" signal when you agree with other employees.

4. Actively listen.

5. Write down others' ideas.

6. Take ideas seriously.

7. Accept others' opinions.

8. Accept differences in others.

9. Express feelings.

10. Recognize feelings.

11. Give tangible rewards.

12. Recognize important events about other's lives.

13. Document highlights (events).

14. Arrange for boss to acknowledge good work.

15. Point out good consequences of another's actions.

16. Spend time with others.

17. Support others' actions.

18. Ask for opinions on how to solve problems.

19. Delegate.

20. Ask for help.

21. Share experiences.

22. Admit you are wrong.

23. Say, "You are right."

24. Repeat compliments from others.

25. Say, "Hi! How are You?"

26. Show constructive concern about performance problems.

27. Shake hands.

28. Smile.

29. Ask about others' interests.

30. Invite someone to join you for coffee.

31. Inquire (with empathy) about someone's family problems.

32. Provide a new piece of equipment.

33. Ask someone to lead all or part of a meeting.

34. Give a teaching assignment.

35. Use an employee's name.

36. Establish and keep follow-up dates.

37. Share information.

38. Give complete reasons for directions.

However, discipline is important. We need self-discipline as a reminder that enhancing others' self-esteem is a twenty-four-hour job. To help me be more consistent in this manner, I have had note pads made with the word appreciation written down the side. I put a box along the side of each of the twelve letters in the word. Each morning I set a goal on how many times I could express my appreciation to someone for his or her contributions to the company. If I reached my goal for that day, I would allow myself the reward I had planned — a dessert after dinner perhaps, or a glass of wine. Something I care about. If I did not reach my goal, I would deny myself my reward.

I also had cards and note pads made with my name on them. No title, just the informal name, Jim Moore. I would send these cards to people I would meet or see doing something right, praising them and thanking them. Not much effort on my part, but a ton of value to the person whose self-esteem I helped enhance.

A very important goal of a leader is be to be consistent in his/her endeavor to keep the environment positive. I have had people tell me, "Oh, I do a great job creating a positive environment, it's just every now and then I have a bad day. Everyone can have a bad day." It usually shocks them when I tell them that they aren't, as leaders, allowed to have a bad day. They are viewed and evaluated by their staffs by the minute. Your people don't really care if you are having a bad day: a momentary slip may take forever to repair. Consistency is important or our people will know we are not sincere, and they will suspect our motives.

When I was in high school, I lived in Punxsutawney, PA. the home of Punxsutawney Phil. On the second day of every February, Phil comes out of his hole to determine if he saw his shadow or not. If Phil saw his shadow we are assured of six more weeks of winter. Of course, if Phil did not see his shadow winter would soon be over. Over three thousand people gather early each February second at Gobblers Knob (I have no idea why it is called that) to cheer the designated celebrity ground hog of that new year. You can just imagine the pride and warmth that must flow through that critter as flash bulbs pop, television cameras roll and thousands cheer. You can also imagine how that ground hog must feel the next day when, at 6:35 a.m., he arises from his burrow and no one is there. It's no wonder the city has to get a new groundhog each year, Old Punxsutawney Phil must die of a disappointed and broken heart, because the attention shown him was only once a year.

Do you know managers who compliment or praise so infrequently it seems like only once a year?

Overcoming The Myth:

You must first buy into the premise that you can not motivate anyone to do anything they do not want to do. If an individual does something against their will because of fear or threat, chances are they were intimidated rather than motivated. Therefore, setting an environment of self-inspiration is the ultimate vehicle toward helping others successfully reach out to achieve the common objective of all.

If you are working within a company, set up advisory groups where membership is rotated. Have one of the key roles of this group be informing management of ways the organization can improve self-esteem practices. Assign the responsibility of quality of life issues to a member of management.

Other factors to put into action to enhance others' self-esteem:

- Reward good work

- Praise loudly – criticize softly

- Respect others as individuals

- Treat others as they want to be treated

- Make everyone feel they are important to the business

- Communicate all news, not just bad

- Ask others their opinion

- Listen – listen – listen

Encourage everyone to use the knowledge they have learned about themselves. As a leader, the single best gift you can give to others is to assist in their achievement of their dreams. Encourage others to have "stratitude," a combination of strategy and attitude. They will fulfill their dreams and objectives if they logically put to work a plan to capitalize on their strengths and improve their limitations. Then they must carry it out with determination to reach those goals. They must have a "never give up" mentality.

The key steps in using "stratitude" are:

1. DECIDE what it is you want.

2. WRITE it down.

3. PLAN how you are going to get it.

4. CHECK it off when you get it.

5. TRACK your results – both good and bad.

Not all your preparations are going to succeed. Keep track of your results and what went wrong so you can correct your mistakes and take alternative action. Conversely, keep careful records of your successes. How and why did you reach your goals? A real champion not only knows why He or She failed, but why He or She was victorious, as well.

> *"Lack of something to feel important about is almost the greatest tragedy a man may have."*
> Arthur E. Morgan

• • • • • •

CHAPTER X

Strategic Thinking
The Myths Of Planning And Instinct

"We don't need a g— d— strategic plan." The words were clear but, as if the executive speaking knew I was in disbelief of what I had just heard, he repeated them again. "We don't need a strategic plan." This time the words were spit out with even more passion than before.

The outburst had been prompted by a group of very upset investors anxious to learn what was going to be done to fix the problems in the company, in which, they had put their capital. They were concerned there was no strategic thinking in place to protect their investment. Even more alarming to the investment group was their worry that the CEO had no plan and, perhaps, was incapable of delivering one.

The CEO was reacting with this anger because he, indeed, had no plan, and hadn't a clue as to how one should be developed. His inability to express a plan and his demonstrative behavior had nothing to do with his capacity to think. He was, by far, one of the most intelligent leaders I had ever met. His frustration was fostered by his management style which, in turn, was driven by his ego.

Personal charm, IQ, dedication, and hard work were wonderful qualities this executive possessed.

Unfortunately, they were not enough to lead his company from the chasm that past management had placed it in. A few limitations were allowed to dominate this CEO and the decisions he made.

64

This leader loved making decisions. These decisions were made from his knowledge, experiences, and basic instincts. High individual intelligence and good basic instinct, both an asset, cannot substitute for the creative collective thinking of the total management team. There must be a broad base of decision making in an organization. The collective reasoning of many will give the needed balance to make decisions that can stand up to the challenges of the new business world.

The eventual acceptance of the strategic direction, by the staff, starts with involvement from the beginning of the process. A lone individual may have a vision, but the dream moves forward with the efforts of the team. A complete understanding of the concept is fundamental while forming a base for strategic thinking. However, knowing what you are is part of the strategic process. A strategic plan must answer three fundamental questions. These questions are:

Who are we?

Where are we going?

How are we going to get there?

Without the answers to these questions there can be no logical action taken within your company. Action toward achieving common, future objectives, or actions directed at improving or extending past successes, should always take into considerations these questions.

As the market place changes few individuals can have all the answers to these questions. A leader must be able to admit they alone do not possess all the solutions and visions needed for planning the futures of their companies. For management to embrace the plan they must feel they are a part of the decision process. Staffs want to believe they have a share in what will effect their lives.

A step by step look a strategic thinking begins with:

Preliminary preparation:

Start with a meeting of all direct reports to the CEO or chief leader of the company.

Include in the meeting other key employees who can contribute. There is no magical number for attendance. I recommend a range of seven to fifteen. Anymore than fifteen may be difficult logistically. Arrange a meeting room away from the office. Leave instructions that only emergency calls will be received.

Have facilitators, from outside the company, conduct your planning sessions. This person should have no emotional or financial concern of the decisions made at the meetings. The facilitator should be experienced and capable to move the meeting along skillfully and tactfully. Facilitators have their own styles and preferences how strategic planning sessions should be designed. I have done many strategic planning meetings for various companies and, as a facilitator, like to use the following rules and outlines.

Rules:

Everyone should: Feel comfortable to speak openly and honestly.

Have an understanding there will be no recriminations from opinions stated.

Do not react to negative comments or criticism.

Do not take comments personally.

Be encouraged to speak.

See to it that no one is monopolizing the conversation.

The CEO/leader should participate as a mere member of the team.

The session:

I like to use the process for planning that includes the following components:

STRATEGIC THINKING PROCESS

Situational Analysis ⟶ External Environment ⟶

Internal Environment ⟶ Vision ⟶ Objective ⟶

Mission Statement ⟶ Strategic Statement ⟶ Tactics

Situational Analysis:

Situational analysis is a bullet point review of past company history and current trends. In this section the question, "What is happening now and what has been the trend?"

Areas to cover:

Past and present sales trends.

Past and present customer counts.

Average sales per customer.

Demographic studies of customers.

Significant expenses.

Competition.

Market share.

Brand awareness.

Product analysis.

Company history.

External Environment:

External environmental factors have an affect on issues the leaders have little or no effect over. These factors will have a direct or indirect influence on your culture, sales, costs, and/ or profits.

Samples of areas covered:

Local, state or federal legislature.

Culture changes, i.e., generation gaps.

Outside organizational issues.

Environmental issues.

Market and demographic shifts.

Internal Environment:

Internal environment is an introspective look at your company's strengths and limitations. I usually like to take the positive first, and review the company's strengths; then I cover the company's limitations. You will find the review of limitations usually takes three times as long as the time spent on strengths. Please keep in mind, when you advance to tactics, that it is important to capitalize on the company strengths and improve on company limitations. This process is much the same as when a leader analyzes his/her own leadership characteristics that we covered in chapter V. It is very important to encourage group participation and honesty while participating in the sessions.

By the time you come to this point in the strategic thinking session, the question "Who are we?" should have been answered.

Situational Analysis—External Environment—Internal Environment

Make up the answers to WHO ARE WE?

Vision:

Where do you see your company in the future? Vision is the gift a leader gives to the people in his/her organization. Vision is the communication of the company's purpose and sense of direction. A vision statement should be written or expressed verbally in such a fashion that everyone in the company will have no difficulty understanding its intent.

A vision must be more than just simplistic. It must be a humanistic position and relate what is important to the company. The vision should express what the company values most. Your vision should outline what future products and/or services your company will excel in. A good vision is one everyone can live with 100 percent of the time.

Objective:

What is it, exactly, you want to accomplish within your company? At this point in the strategic thinking session one or, the most, two objectives should be determined.

Examples of a leader's objective for the strategic plan could be:

> We want to be a $500,000,000 company with 2000 stores by _____

> We want to have earnings of _____ with a stock price of _____

> We want to generate a positive cash flow of _____

For some reason the objective part of the strategic thinking process seems to be a large hurdle for many executives to get over. I work with many leaders in these sessions that want to wait until all the various sections, including tactics, are completed before objectives are discussed. I simply explain that before going forward we must know what our target is before we can fire any shots.

Mission Statement:

As a leader, you will want to develop a mission statement that describes how everyone in the company will routinely behave. While the vision statement reflects the leader's dreams; the mission statement will relate how that vision works on a day-today basis. The mission statement should describe what the company values the most. Generally, the factors covered in the mission statement are either **quality of product, service delivered,** or **value perceived.** Many companies I work with feel that **employee treatment** is equally important.

My mission for my company, Moore Ideas Incorporated, is as follows: "To discover what keeps leaders awake at night, and help provide solutions." This simple statement did not come to me easy. A lot of thought, and many rewrites occurred before I was satisfied with the final result.

The question "Where are going?" should be answered when you arrive at this point in the strategic thinking process.

Situational Analysis—External Environment—Internal Environment

WHO ARE WE?

Vision Statement ———— Objective ———— Mission Statement

Make up the answers to WHERE ARE WE GOING?

Strategic Statement:

Often, at this point in the strategic thinking process, many of my clients are eager to get to the tactics. I, however, believe that time should be taken to think about a simple statement that describes how the mission will be executed.

Consider my company's strategic statement: "To research current and future challenges for leaders of the hospitality industry, and communicate potential solutions through keynote speeches, consulting, and publications."

Your strategic statement supports your reason for being by expressing how strategically you would carry out your mission. As the mission statement reflects the leader's dreams the strategic statement outlines how these dreams will be fulfilled. Perhaps it would be beneficial to dissect the Moore Ideas mission statement.

"<u>To discover</u> (research) <u>what keeps leaders</u> (present and prospective clients in the restaurant, hotel, and related foodservice businesses)<u> awake at night</u> (the serious problems that affect profits and growth) <u>and help provide solutions</u>." (study existing problems and future trends. Communicate solutions with my talks, consulting and books).

Tactics:

Tactics are the individual action steps taken in order for the objective to be reached. These tactics should be measured against the vision and mission to guarantee the maintenance of the company's values and integrity. For example, your company's objective is to improve cash flow by 50 percent. Your mission, then, is to provide the best possible service in your business segment, or reduce costs, streamline production, etc..

You have decided, strategically, that the best approach, to reach your cash flow objective, is through increased market share. A tactic to reduce service staff by 10 percent would help cash flow in the short term but, downsizing staff could be counter to the company's mission and strategy.

Each tactic should address the following questions:

What goal do you want to reach?

What action will you take?

What will be the result of your action?

When will the action be implemented?

When will the tactic be completed?

Who will be responsible?

71

Tactics are the last thing done in the strategic thinking process. It is a myth that good leaders do not have time to spend "Sitting around all day in meetings when there are things to be done." Action taken without thought is often misdirected.

I am sure that the knights of old had a plan, on how to get the dragon out of the cave, instead of charging into the darkness to meet their prey head on.

Many leaders incorrectly think they have obtained success because of their ability to make fast decisions. They are so anxious to solve a problem; they want to execute the tactics before all the other important factors are considered.

Overcoming the myth:

Insight and instinct are wonderful assets of leaders, when used sensibly. Instinct must be tempered with the company's values and strategic thinking. A good strategic plan will always be a useful and valuable tool for the decisive leader with good common sense.

THE STRATEGIC ORBIT

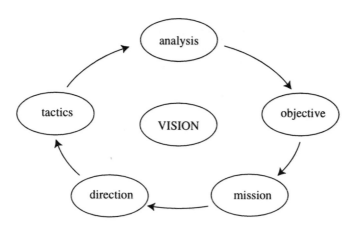

"The sign of an intelligent people is their ability
to control emotions by the application of reason."
Marya Mannes

Chapter XI

• • • • • • •

The Turn-Around Leader
Destroying The Myths That
Prevent Improvements

I did not set out to become a turn-around specialist, it just happened. My career of fixing sick restaurants and restaurant companies started rather innocently. In 1963, my company asked me to return to Chicago, Illinois, to take over one of their largest restaurants. The reason for the move was clear. The restaurant was performing poorly. Sales and profits had declined the past several years. I got a sense of the problem on my first day. The general manager, who I was replacing, greeted me and immediately announced he would show me what was most important for me to know about that restaurant.

I should digress for a moment to tell you a little about this restaurant. It was one of Stouffer's larger units, with over 1,000 dining seats in eight different dining rooms. The restaurant covered three floors of the Madison Building in downtown Chicago. The restaurant had a management staff of ten and approximately 200 cooks, pantry servers, and service personnel. A busy lunch would mean serving 3,800 lunches, and we would serve over 2,500 dinners on shopping nights.

Back to "The most important thing I needed to know about the restaurant." The present general manager led me from the office, located on the mezzanine, to the main dining room. We continued down, yet another floor, to the men's grill. Men's grilles were very popular until legislation determined they were discriminatory.

We continued our journey into the kitchen, past the bakery station where he opened the door to a boiler room. In an exaggerated manner, the general manager pointed at two plumbers 'snakes' used to clear drains. "This is the most important thing you will need to know how to do in this operation, because the drains are always backing up." "You've got to be kidding me," I replied. "Don't you have a maintenance man on the staff?" He answered "Well – yes we do." "Then from now on he does his best to prevent the drains from backing up and, if they do, he will clear them. I will devote my time to finding out how we can increase the customer counts by 20 percent."

I learned, soon after, that this general manager had difficulty with priorities. He felt if he was not physically working he was not accomplishing anything. When he hadn't worked hard, doing hourly work, he felt incomplete.

It did not take me long to discover what was causing the sales and profit declines in this restaurant.

1. Lack of respect for management.

2. Running out of food early each meal period.

3, High food costs.

4. Server morale was low because of the food "run-outs," (unavailable product), and low tips because of customer dissatisfaction.

Through a change of some key management personnel, improved communications with the cooks and pantry servers concerning food cost goals, and my hands on management of production forecasts (rather than drain clearing), we turned the restaurant into a positive sales and profit trend in three months.

It is a myth that it takes very special talents to be a turn-around specialist. It takes talent, of course, but none any different than what a good leader would already possess. The circumstances have to be right as well. I am very proud of all my turn-around successes. However, I must admit, as challenging as each turn-around assignment is, it is much more difficult to manage a going concern year in and year out. I learned early in my career if you are good at what you do, and are faced with a turn-around challenge, chances are you will follow mediocre management. After all, how did it get messed up in the first place? But try competing against yourself each fiscal year. The greatest challenge to a leader is continuing to meet improvement expectations each year.

What skills do you need to become recognized as a turn-around expert?

1. Discover or be assigned to follow poor or mediocre managers/leaders

2. Love of challenges

3. Good common sense

4. Have courage, it's always lonely for awhile

5. Follow the seven rules of turn-around leadership

Follow mediocre management: good leaders or, a "good enough" leader who did not adequately adapt to changing conditions seldom causes The need for vast improvement.

Have a love for challenges: Stress and risk taking are parts of being a leader that make you happy.

Good common sense: You will, generally, find there is a one-to-three-month time period while assessing the situation where instincts will play an important role.

Courage to go it alone: It is always lonely until you get a few successes behind you. As the victories occur, the allies increase.

Able to follow the seven rules of turn-around leadership: The following all the rules of leading turn-around situations I have learned through the years:

Rule # One – Assess the situation before acting.

It was June 4, 1983. My boss, Vince Kikugawa, called to ask me to accept "The greatest turn-around challenge of your life." Vince wanted me to become the chief operator for a group of Mexican restaurants located on both coasts of the United States. The company wanted to expand its Mexican chain. Senior management felt there was still a window of opportunity remaining for growth in the Northeast. Frankly, I was not excited, about still, another challenge of this magnitude having performed numerous successful turn-arounds in the past. I loved what I was doing, running a chain of steak houses. We had just completed a year where we opened twelve restaurants in eleven months, and I was looking forward to year of normalcy. Besides, I knew nothing about running Mexican restaurants. But Vince was not someone you said no to. So in early July, I took over a chain of Mexican restaurants, located on two coasts, with sub-par profit results.

My first step was to request research funds. I wanted to know what potential and present customers expected of Mexican restaurants. It was equally important to understand how the potential (non-user) customer perceived us as well as how our present customer (user) saw us.

We did the research quickly, and the following is what we uncovered:

MEXICAN RESTAURANTS

Expectation	Evaluation
• Entrees priced under $5.00	• We averaged $6.00 – $7.00
• Great tasting margaritas	• Did not have much tequila in ours
• Eat and out in 45 minutes	• One hour plus
• Colorful atmosphere	• Drab / boring
• Fun, lively servers	• Matched up well

I have found that doing research is easy if you have the capital to pay for it. It's the correct analytical assessment of the data that is difficult and critical. You, as the leader, can get assistance analyzing the data and developing the necessary action steps. But your the final conclusions must come from within. The following are the action steps we took after considering the research conclusions:

1. Lowed selected entree prices – UN-bundled items from the price. Items such as salads, sour cream, guacamole were priced separately.

2. Changed the margarita recipe and enforced the specifications.

3. Transferred a service director from another division who had the ability to capitalize on our friendly service staff. This person was energetic and flexible. She could change the present service standards from the slower dinner house style, presently in place, to a faster more casual service. Just as importantly she could sell it to the present servers.

4. We could not afford the capital to renovate the restaurants so we filled the lobbies with hundreds of colorful balloons and ribbons.

    Changed uniforms from the traditional white shirt and black pants to colorful dresses and shirts.

    Designed a colorful paper menu that customers could take home with them.

5. Capitalized on our present servers by emphasizing songs, fun, and unique service. Each guest received a tiny ice cream cone filled with a colorful sherbet when the check was presented.

The bottom-line? Past management ran a Mexican restaurant like a formal dinner house. We changed to a concept the customers told us they wanted.

Then, after we felt we were operating well, we started to advertise using radio as the principal medium. The results were extremely positive. Over a two year period:

Guest counts	+22%
Sales	+32%
Profits	+42%

These results stemmed from the <u>research</u>, correct assessment of the data, and aggressive action.

RULE # TWO – "Have the right horses."

One of my dad's favorite expressions was "In order to win consistently—you had to have the right horses in all the right spots." The fact he was a football coach might make you wonder what in the world was he talking about? As a little boy, sitting around the kitchen table, I was quick to learn Dad was using that term to remind himself, and anyone else who would listen, you must have good players in the right positions in order to win. My Dad was a master at assessing young men's talents and placing them where their skills would be best utilized to compliment the team.

As a leader, in turn-around situations, evaluating the type of skills individuals need is a top priority. Then you must determine if that talent in the organization presently and, if there are specific key roles that need to be filled quickly. It is always best to keep as many of the existing management on board as possible.

You lose time and resources if the team must be replaced. I have always prided myself as possessing the ability to improve and develop people to meet the challenges of new objectives. However, that pride on occasions caused me to make some mistakes. There will be individuals within the company who are insecure and afraid of change, or who's egos will not allow them to be part of the new team. These people should be weeded out quickly. There were a few times I waited too long to make those tough decisions and it caused us precious time and productivity.

Previously I have talked about peoples needs, strengths and limitations. A good leader finds out as much as he/she can about all the key management as quickly as possible. Put existing people in important positions that highlight their skills. Then bring in 'out-siders' to fill the need your existing staff can not fulfill. Make sure that the people you bring into the company will fit in with your existing staff and culture.

RULE # THREE – Hire and hold great employees.

One of the greatest challenges a leader has today is finding and maintaining an excellent employee base. Leaders, in order to be effective, must have inspired, enthusiastic people who are excited about the company's objectives.

Finding Great Help:

Between 1965 and 1976 there were 44.6 million babies born. This birth rate compares to 77.6 million born between 1946 - 1964. That is 42.5 percent less births in the decade that is expected to provide your workers today.

If you work in retail, food service, housing or related service industries you know how critical the pool of 21 - 35 year-olds are to satisfying your hiring needs. But, as if having a smaller base of an employee pool to operate from isn't enough, the workers within that pool have become exceptionally mobile. Different from past generations, where security was an important priority, this generation is looking for a experiences that offer variety. So, if you are still offering the same building, hours, experiences routinely, you are not meeting the needs of this generation of workers.

In order to provide solutions for hiring and maintaining great employees a leader must have an understanding of the values of this group. The characteristics of the generation x group are:

- They get bored easily – want a variety of experiences and challenges.

- Entrepreneurial – willing to take risks, and to be self-taught.

- Less loyal – after watching their parents get downsized after many years of service to their companies, they have a distrust for establishments.

- Want more interesting and exciting jobs – call most food service jobs "McJobs."

- Optimistic about achieving their personal goals as long as they can control their fate, but cynical about the future – A recent study of graduating seniors out of colleges indicated they would rather manage their own retirement funds and medical insurance. They do not believe Medicare and social security will be there when they will need them.

- Independent but, at the same time, family oriented – while believing they must take control of their own destiny, the Generation X ER is becoming more family-oriented than your workers' in past decades. Spending time with the family has moved high on the new workers priority of needs.

- Very well educated – especially in the area of technology.

Considering the uniqueness of this new generation, what can you do to hire and hold them in your organization? Start building your reputation as the employer of choice by being visible at high schools and colleges. Advertise and sponsor high visibility activities. Hire a student to be your representative on campus, something Nike does very well. Speak in classes. Sponsor job fairs. Have receptions for school clubs. Give schools tours of your business. Offer tuition and book subsidies for grade achievement. Dick Clark's American Bandstand restaurants utilize this program very successfully. Offer job mobility within your company. Let people work with different co-workers and managers. Offer flexible and/or different hours. Cross train; it will also increase productivity.

Offer not only managerial advancement , but entrepreneurial opportunities as well. In some cases, becoming a franchisee is a possibility. Create fun, friendly, family environments. Celebrate things and do things together. Build up loyalty from within; i.e., the working team will be looked at as a family unit. Allow time off for family events. Let people leave and return to work. Some companies are very rigid about this, but times have changed. Grant time off for mini sabbaticals. Mix the boring parts of work with the more exciting or interesting tasks.

Have employee and customer advisory councils, and listen to what they have to say. A speaker friend of mine, Danny Cox, told me about his friend, Stew Leonard's, dairy store. The largest sales producing dairy store in the United Sates, and perhaps the World. The suggestion box is placed where both employees and customers can deposit suggestions. Every day at 8:30 am the box is emptied. By 10:00 am all suggestion are typed and presented to management for discussion at that day's staff meeting.

Danny tells me that the most important part of this procedure is management's concern that all suggestions are looked at as to how they can be utilized, rather than how they can be rejected.

Teach employees how to utilize the trust you have given them. Give them examples and case studies of situations that need solved, and tell them to come up with creative solutions.

Rule # Four – Rewards and recognition are as important as remuneration.

If you have great employees, and are doing everything you can to reward and recognize them, you may still lose them to someone else who is willing to pay more. You should pay competitive wages, but paying well is not enough to maintain employees. There must be a balance of praise, recognition, opportunity, variety, and compensation.

Low-Cost Ways To Reward Your People:

- Praise loudly – criticize softly.

- Refrain from using the sandwich approach to criticize. Praise ——— Criticize ——— Praise

- Praise people ASAP – don't wait.

- Instead of employee-of-the-month parking spaces, wash their car while they work.

- Give out coupons for cookies, movies, gas, car washes, etc.

- Pay dry-cleaning bills.

- Day care provisions – pay part of the cost, or have on premise.

- Arrange trade outs with other businesses. For example a restaurant might trade free meals for free books for their employees.

- Give small gifts to employees. The Stouffer Corporation gave my wife and I a picture frame when our first child was born. It made me feel like a valued member of the company. Unfortunately, the company discontinued this policy because "we were growing so fast it became unwieldy and too costly." My thoughts at the time were: if we were growing so fast, weren't we making more money, as well?

- When you offer an incentive for specific goals – always pay up. I have seen, over and over, leaders and Company boards, make specific incentive plans, only to discount the payout for various reasons. Even if the rationale has a modicum of merit; pay what was promised. The negative affects are too damaging when this approach is taken.

RULE # FIVE – Set performance improvement goals.

Earlier in this book I covered the importance of teaching everyone in the organization the company's basic function. A businesses basic function is to create and keep customers. A leader's basic function, therefore, is also to create and keep customers. Not only does the company exist to meet the needs of their customers, but to provide for the human needs of their employees. Needs like recognition, opportunity, and belonging are just a step behind the basic needs of food, clothing, and shelter that must be satisfied by the company's leaders.

Businesses succeed or fail because of people. People make the products, and people buy those products and services the company provides.

Previously it was pointed out that making a profit was the objective of the company, not its basic function. Now we know it is also not why a company exists. Leaders exist, therefore, to fulfill the basic needs of their people.

It does not, however, take a turn-around situation to draw attention to the fact that business cannot exist without profit. Profit is essential for a leader and a company to survive. A company needs profit in order to grow. It also needs profit in order to measure its productivity. In a turn-around situation, the ultimate measure is how the profitability performs, against your base. (Previous profit and profit objectives)

The more you are able to fulfill the needs of your employees and customers; the higher the profits will be. Profit improvements co-exist with the productivity improvements of the people in the organization.

By developing a culture that communicates the company's reason for being and its basic function, the turn-around leader may concentrate on what it will take to realize improved profits: Many of these areas are outlined below:

5-1. Develop standards and goals for result improvements

5-2. Determine the measurement by which the results will be evaluated

5-3. Decide the specifications needed for key roles in the company

5-4. Determine the results needed from those key positions

5-5. Get the right people in place

5-6. Determine how you will keep on top of the results as they progress.

5-7. Decide how you will communicate the results

RULE # SIX – Be willing to deal with company politics and sacred cows.

In practically every turn-around challenge; the leader will be faced with certain political situations and sacred cows.

Sacred Cows:

For a example a chef doesn't want his/her recipe changed because it will lower the quality of his creation, at least in his eyes. She/he refuses to see, through the years, that customer's tastes have changed. Customers may want less fat, fewer calories, less sweetness of taste, etc. But because of egotism, insecurity, or pride of authorship the chef will fight every suggestion to change. The resistance to change a recipe is this chef's sacred cow.

Sacred cows can be almost anything. A few years back I was contacted by the founder of a small steak-house chain. He asked if I would have lunch with him. During our meal he asked me if I would consider running his company for him. He was in need of a major turn-around. I asked him a number of question which he readily answered. Just before the meal was over I asked, "What sacred cows do you have in your organization?" The question startled him for a second, but eventually he replied that he had several relatives in key positions and they could not be changed under any circumstance. I politely declined his offer. A turn-around leader must be able to eliminate all negative sacred cows. But all sacred cows aren't bad.

I was asked to facilitate a leadership / planning session for Lawry's Prime Rib restaurants, based in Pasadena, California. The CEO's, Mr. John Frank II, objective was to eliminate the sacred cows in the company.

During our fact-finding session it became clear to me that all of their scared cows were not necessarily bad. Their mission (not quoted exactly) is to serve the finest quality food available. Therefore, they specify the highest quality prime rib you can purchase, USDA prime. Many in the company consider this specification a sacred cow; however, serving the very best was how Lawry's wanted to run their company. Maintaining high standards is a quality value of the company, not a sacred cow.

Politics:

Generally, company politics is when people say and do subtle things to harm someone else's reputation. They usually do these things for their own personal gain. Politics, in a company, occurs when the leader allows it to happen. A turn-around leader will not have the luxury of time to hope that those applying company politics will mature or go away. The leader must face these matters boldly, quickly, and with frankness. Bring to the attention of those responsible the fact that you know what is going on, and you will not tolerate it. As you seek out your own dragons to slay you will need a well-coordinated team supporting your quest.

RULE # SEVEN – Walk the talk.

A few years back I was running a division for a food-service company undergoing a change of leadership. The challenges that faced our new leader created the need for an outstanding turn-around specialist. I didn't know very much about our new leader but, shortly after taking over, he released a six-page document describing "What he was all about."

Well, I can tell you, I was impressed. It was a beautifully written description of his values, philosophies, and management style.

I was so impressed with the document I carried it with me, in my day planner. Every now and then I would read it over again, hoping to learn from the principles this wonderful paper revealed. I gave copies to my staff and reviewed it with them before our meetings.

It was not long, however, before I discovered this beautifully written concept was a farce. The man did almost everything the opposite to what was written. I knew we had a serious problem, and our turn-around was in jeopardy, when my staff started teasing me about the document. Soon I stopped carrying the papers around with me. I suspect our leader had seen an article somewhere he like, and copied it for his own use.

By not walking his talk he not only did not succeed in quickly turning around the company, he made things much worse.

"The highest use of capital is not to make more money,
but to make money do more for the betterment of life."
Henry Ford

CHAPTER XII

• • • • • • •

Tough Enough For Love

The Myth That You Have To Be
Hard Nosed To Lead

There are many differences of opinion as to what are the most effective philosophy and demeanor of a highly effective leader. This controversy is accentuated when some successful business people write books promoting how they have been a winner by being "mean." Meanness and ruthlessness can produce short-term rewards, but this is not leadership. It's fear and intimidation. Albert J. Dunlap has written a book called "Mean Business" in which he points out that a tough-minded leader must:

1. Get the right management team.

2. Cut the flab out of the organization.

3. Focus on the most profitable areas.

4. Plan a route to a bright future.

Sounds like good common sense to me. But do you really have to be a mean person to execute that plan?

Mr. Dunlap takes a hard-nosed approach to protecting the shareholders' interest. I agree with that position. Tough-minded leadership means:

1. Not wasting the shareholders' assets.

2. Never bending on the company's policies of quality and service standards.

3. Operating with the highest integrity.

4. Rigidly obeying all laws and regulations.

5. Being tough enough to set an atmosphere of caring so others can have the self-esteem needed to do their very best.

As in the past, the beliefs, feelings, attitudes and behaviors of the workers tend to change. We see more and more that the needs of management and staff are shifting. No longer are career, money, security and power among the top needs of middle management. Family and quality of life have taken the prominent positions as the need priorities.

The inner spirit of today's worker must be in tune with that of its leaders. The environment that leaders create for others must be built on love, compassion and caring. The workers of tomorrow will not be loyal to a company, but will support and trust an individual or family. These future workers will react poorly to a discipline-based management. You have to have a tough-minded discipline but, by tough, I mean you have to be tough in defending your company's standards and your company's specifications. You have to be tough in protecting the rights and the safety of your guests and your employees. You have to be tough in protecting your own ethics.

When I got started in the restaurant business, they told me that to be an effective leader I had to be a tough, hard-nosed, take-no-prisoners type of manager. So I became a tough, hard-nosed, take no-prisoners type of manager and I failed miserably. At one point in my life, I didn't want to go to work. I was just dragging around every morning. Have you ever felt that way? I would sit there with coffee at the breakfast table, not wanting to get up and get in that car and go to work. My youngest daughter, Rebecca, must have recognized that something was wrong. Becca was around six years old. She was sitting there with me at the table, her pigtails sticking out, freckles all over her face. When she looked at me she said, "Daddy, what I like about you is you don't take all the love with you when you go away."

Well, I thought about that all the way to work. She was right, I didn't take all the love with me when I went. I left love behind for my children; in fact, I left all my love behind for my children! I took nothing with me to work, and by the time I got to my office I had decided that I was going to change the way I thought about these matters and, therefore, change my actions and, by changing my actions, change the results of my company.

I put a caring, compassionate, loving relationship into my business. One that wanted other people's ideas. I brought them all together as a team, and with the help of a six-year-old little girl, we went on to five straight years of record sales and profit. Our 'dragons' were slain that day because we replaced myth with compassion.

I didn't realize what kind of an effect this change would have on me until many years later. In Irvine, California I was preparing a barbecue on a Fourth of July weekend. I noticed that the Irvine police had pulled up in front of my house. Immediately I thought, "What did I do?" I thought back on the last three or four weeks and took an inventory of my actions. I thought, "I didn't do anything!" So I did what any red-blooded American husband would do, I pointed at my wife! And she said, "I didn't do anything!" Now the police were at out our front door, but they were much too polite, and I knew something was wrong. The police informed me that my oldest son, Bobby, had died in his sleep the night before. Oh, the shock! I had never felt pain like that before. I loved that boy so much. I thought my life was now over...everything was over for me. I didn't think I was going to be able to go on, but some how you do.

You have to go on and, after awhile, I did. I went back to work, but I was only half there. I was just going through the motions. Standing in our restaurant in Huntington Beach one day, a young busboy by the name of Carlos came up and said, "Mr. Jim, I'm sorry." Carlos also said "Are you in much pain?" I could only nod my head. He went on to say, "Did your son leave you any good memories?" "Well, as a matter of fact, Carlos, Bobby left me a lot of wonderful memories," I replied.

"Well, Mr. Jim, I'm sure that someday all of those wonderful memories will take the place of all that pain and sorrow you now have." It was at that moment that I realized that Bobby hadn't taken all of his love with him when he'd gone. Bobby had left behind his love in those wonderful memories I have of him. With the help of a six-year-old little girl, we were able to create a caring, concerned, compassionate, loving environment that allowed a busboy to give direction to the president of a company. A busboy gave leadership to the president!

About two weeks later, I received a call from my youngest son, Scott, who said he'd been thinking about it and said, "Dad, I think we ought to give Bobby's car to Elizabeth." Well, Bobby's car was brand new and paid for. Bobby loved his sister Elizabeth, who was a beautiful, talented, but starving artist in West Los Angeles. Bobby loved her and he loved to tease her, so I thought it was only appropriate that she get the car. I called Elizabeth and she came out to the house. We cleaned up the car. In the trunk I found 14 large Nike posters that said, "Just do it!" Bobby loved that poster. He wrestled for the University of Arizona, and he loved that slogan. "Just do it." "Just do it." He had those signs all over the walls in his room.

When Elizabeth was ready to go, I gave her the auto's documentation. I said, "Watch for a special California license plate that Bobby had ordered." Six weeks later, the doorbell rang on a Saturday morning, and there was Elizabeth. She said, "He's still teasing me, Dad!" She pulled out from behind her back a license plate that said **I DO IT**. "Can you see me driving up and down the LA freeways with this behind my car?" I said, "No, I really can't see that, but I can see one angel up there bent over in hilarious laughter!"

You need to put love into your business life as well as your personal life. There are so many people out there looking to you for that leadership, care and compassion. You never know when it's going to come back and reward you. By dispelling the "mean" myths of leadership, and implementing the action steps outlined in this book, I was able to move my career forward. If you implement these action steps, you can take your career beyond your wildest imagination! All you have to do is change the way you think and, therefore, change your action. By changing your actions you can change the world.

Overcoming The Myth:

Have faith that a disciplined organization does not represent a "mean" organization. In fact, having faith is an important ingredient for successful leaders. Every truly effective person I've ever known has had a strong personal faith. They have had belief in themselves, but also a belief that there is some wondrous power that created human beings to be good, and to live a life that would contribute to others. This belief is like a strong foundation that represents your total character, and what you stand for in life. Upon this foundation are the building blocks that simulate your life. These building blocks are called TOLERANCE – KINDNESS – COMPASSION – CARING – CONCERN – MORALITY – and INTEGRITY.

These building blocks, when supported by a strong personal faith, form the basis for LOVE. These important blocks become your life, and will guide you toward developing into the person whom others will look to for leadership.

"The supreme happiness of life is the
conviction that we are loved."
Victor Hugo

CONCLUSION

●●●●●●●

M yths can be a wonderful source of entertainment in our lives: myths prompted by recalling the adventurous stories told to us by our parents, or recalling the times spent in movies living our lives through heroes and heroines we watched on the motion picture screen. These times would not have had the magic that so excited us were it not for myths.

In the business world myth often confuses the need to keep current, or to do what is right. We use myth to hide our insecurities. We also use myth as an ego base that constantly needs gratification. In a marketplace that thrives on change, and is filled with competitors, myths can be a mortal enemy. Our mythical dragons must be slain. Leaders of today will achieve their 'knighthood' through defeating the challenges of tomorrow.

The leaders of the future will know the difference between managing and leading. Leaders will use the fundamentals of management to keep the organization functioning in a tight and efficient manner. Anticipation and problem solving will be skills utilized by everyone in the organization. The solutions will not be second- guessed by the real leaders of tomorrow. Successful leaders of the future will use the collective creative vision of all their constituents, and will be willing to stand behind these visions when the road starts getting bumpy. Risks must be taken in order to enact change, but risk should not be taken until all the facts have been carefully evaluated.

Mistakes happen to humans even when they are as careful and thorough as possible. Dwelling on our mistakes, or even worse, inaction is the first ingredient in the recipe for incompetence.

Leaders are rewarded for their positive results that occur due to visions that are implemented regardless of the personal ramifications of the risk elements. Regardless of the kind of business you practice, the principle foundation for that business must center on the customer. How well you practice creating and keeping your customers will be, far and away, the most important factor on the amount of profit you make. Making a profit is your validation that all the leaders in your organization successfully focused on creating and keeping their customers first.

True leaders share responsibility. They realize that they alone can not carry the company's mission. Leaders are aware that it takes everyone pulling together in a common interest that brings visions to fruition.

Leaders see that training is a critical part of their operation. Training should not be a line item expense to cut the first time sales get a little soft. Training is an on-going function. True leaders instill the skills of leadership in every person in the organization. People with a high sense of worth do a superior job.

A leader's role is to see that acts of promoting others' self-esteem are carried by all within the organization. Leaders develop an environment that fosters the praise of individual accomplishments.

Vince Kikugawa believed that "PRIDE BEFORE PROFIT" would be his theme and motto for success. Vince lived his motto every day. Vince felt that enhancing others sense of self-worth would produce the results that made him look good and, hence, increase his self-esteem. It worked.

A mixture of good common sense with your well thought out plans is a valuable asset. Your decisions are enhanced when your values are combined with strategic thinking. Instinct and a strategic sense become powerful allies when united.

A turn-around leader uses his/her talents to communicate the company's basic function, reason for being, and profit goals, and use his/her skills aggressively to alter the present trend or situation. A turn-around leader loves challenges, has good instincts, courage, and is a believer in the 'Seven rules of turn-around leadership."

Toughness is often misinterpreted in business circles. You hear stories of ruthlessness, cold and calculating tales of downsizing blind to human dignity. Leaders must be tough. They need to be rigid in the defense of the company's standards and specifications. Leaders cannot bend when operating under the rules, guidelines, and laws of our nation. Tough-minded leaders have the courage to be ethical at all times, and set an example for others to live by.

More importantly leaders, while following the standards outlined above, must have the courage to love and to be compassionate. The sense that all within your group has a common affection for the results contributed by others, leaves a mark on your destiny forever.

May the enthusiasm generated by you, as a leader of our future, create the energy of greatness carried by many others for decades to come. Your greatness will be enhanced by overcoming the many myths bedeviling today's business world. You will be successful, but **FIRST YOU MUST SLAY THE DRAGON.**

"What is written without effort is in general read without pleasure."
Samuel Johnson